FRANKLIN PARK PUBLIC LIBRARY

FRANKLIN PARK, ILL.

Each borrower is held responsible for all library material drawn on his card and for fines accruing on the same. No material will be issued until such fine has been paid.

All injuries to library material beyond reasonable wear and all losses shall be made good to the satisfaction of the Librarian.

Replacement costs will be
billed after **42 days** overdue.

HEDY LAMARR

DISCOVER THE LIFE OF AN INVENTOR

Ann Gaines

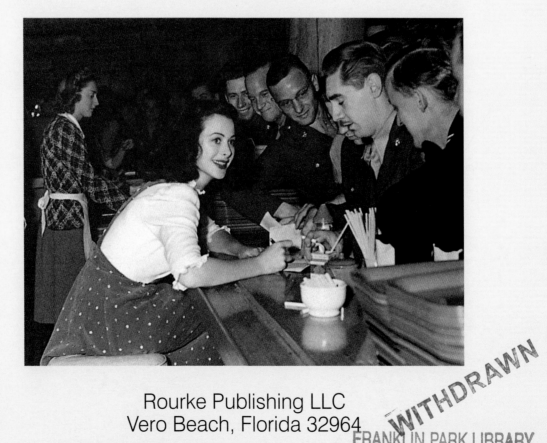

Rourke Publishing LLC
Vero Beach, Florida 32964

www.rourkepublishing.com

PHOTO CREDITS:
Anthony Loder, ©Archive Photo, Gabriel Della Fave

EDITORIAL SERVICES:
Pamela Schroeder

J-B
LAMARR
296-5682

Library of Congress Cataloging-in-Publication Data

Gaines, Ann.
  Hedy Lamarr / Ann Gaines
    p. c. — (Discover the life of an inventor)
  Includes bibliographical references and index.
  ISBN 1-58952-119-6
   1. Lamarr, Hedy, 1915-2000—Juvenile literature. 2. Spread spectrum communications.—Juvenile literature. 3. Actresses—United States—Biography—Juvenile literature. [1. Lamarr, hedy, 1915-2000. 2. Telecommunication—Biography. 3. Inventors. 4. Actors and actresses.] I. Title.

TK5102.56.L35 G34 2001
621.382'092—dc21
[B]   2001019378

Printed in the USA

TABLE OF CONTENTS

HEDY LAMARR AND HER INVENTION

Hedy Lamarr was a movie star and inventor. During her lifetime, most people knew her from her movies of the 1930s and 1940s. Few knew of her idea for guiding **torpedoes**. Torpedoes are bombs used in war. They have motors and move through water.

Her invention also helped to bring about **wireless phones** and pagers.

Hedy is shown here with actor Jimmy Stewart.

FROM HEDWIG TO HEDY LAMARR

Hedwig Kiesler was born November 9, 1914, in Vienna, Austria. Her family called her "Hedy." She became a movie star in Austria while still a teenager. When she was 19, she married Fritz Mandl. His company built guns and torpedoes.

In 1937 Hedy left her husband. She moved to California. In Hollywood, she became a movie star called Hedy Lamarr.

Hedy Lamarr as a young girl in Austria

HEDY LAMARR WANTS TO HELP

In 1939 World War II began in Europe. Germany, Italy, and Japan fought together on one side. Soon the United States joined other countries in fighting against them.

Hedy wanted to help the U.S. fight the war. She knew a lot of the battles would be fought at sea. While married to Fritz Mandl, she had learned about torpedoes. She tried to think of a way to improve them.

Hedy talks with a group of servicemen.

THE PROBLEM WITH TORPEDOES

Hedy knew there was a problem with torpedoes. Some torpedoes were guided by radio signals from the firing ship or **submarine**.

However, enemy ships could hear the radio signals sent from the firing ship. They could stop the radio signal from reaching the torpedo. Then the torpedo could not be guided. It would not hit its target.

Radio operators listen for signals.

THREE IMPORTANT IDEAS

Hedy knew how to hide signals sent from a ship to its torpedo. The ship could quickly flip from one radio channel to another. Then the enemy would not hear the signals.

She also knew how to help the signal from the ship reach the torpedo's radio. Both radios had to change channels together.

A torpedo strikes a ship.

She asked George Antheil to work with her. He had written music for **player pianos**. Player pianos play themselves. A roll of paper punched with holes tells the piano what notes to play. It also tells the piano when to play them.

George had an idea. A roll of paper with holes could tell a radio how to change channels. Both radios would have **identical** rolls of paper. They would change channels together.

A player piano does not need a person to play the keys

THE SECRET COMMUNICATION SYSTEM

Hedy and George received a **patent** for their invention in 1942. They called it the Secret Communication System.

However, the U.S. Navy did not use their idea. It cost too much to change torpedoes during World War II. Hedy helped the U.S. fight the war in other ways. She raised money for the war by selling **bonds**.

A naval crew learns about torpedo communication.

Hedy and George stopped working on their idea. But it did not go away. In 1962 the Navy finally used their invention. They put it on their ships.

Today their idea is called channel hopping. The U. S. uses channel hopping when it sends signals by **satellite**. It keeps secret messages from being understood. It is also used in the Internet.

Hedy Lamarr on the cover of an invention magazine

The Technology of Tennis • Why Things Bite Back

AMERICAN HERITAGE OF

Invention & Technology

SPRING 1997 • VOLUME 12/NUMBER 4

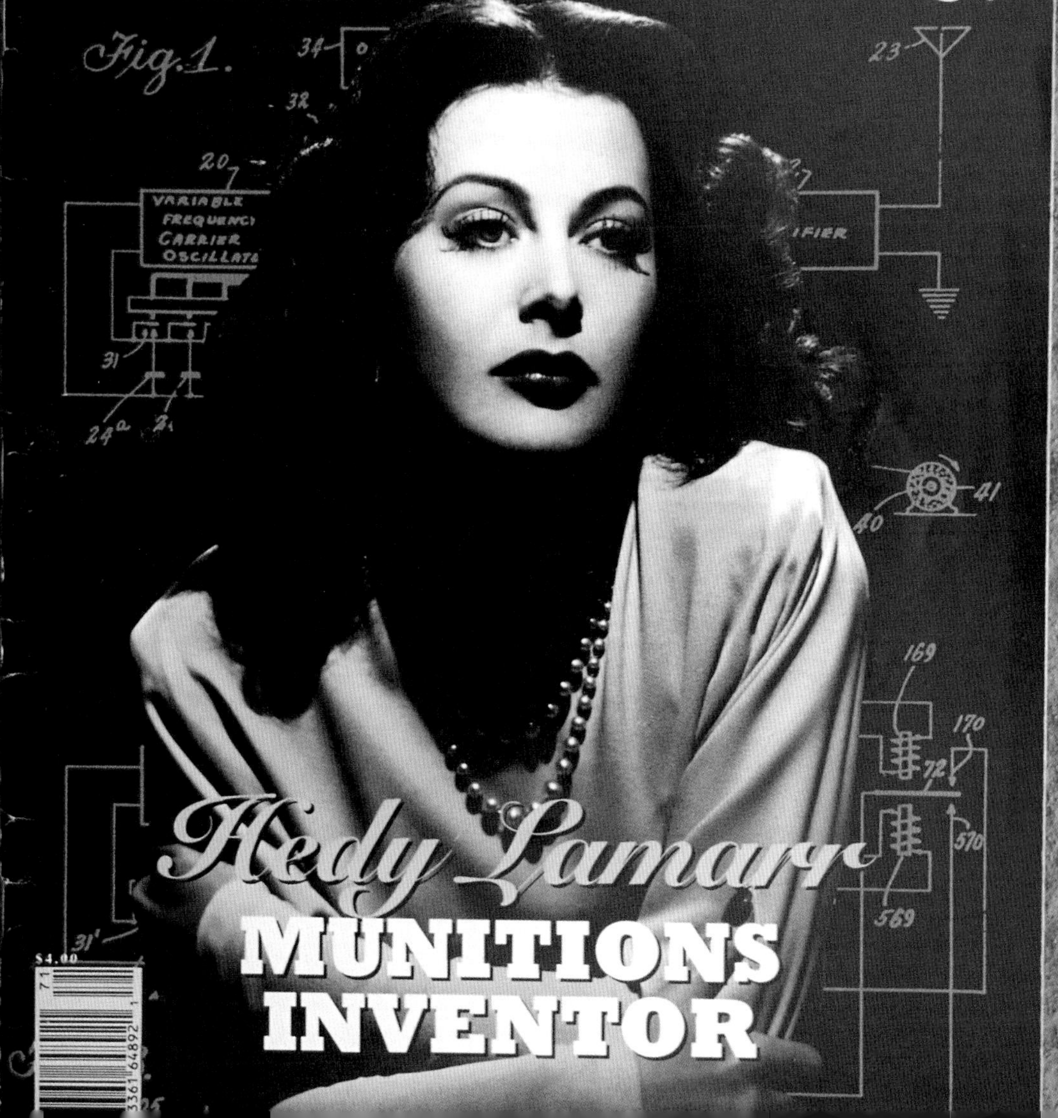
Fig. 1.
VARIABLE FREQUENCY CARRIER OSCILLATOR
IFIER
23
34
32
20
31
24a
41
40
169
170
72
570
569
31'

Hedy Lamarr
MUNITIONS INVENTOR

REMEMBERING HEDY LAMARR

When Hedy was more than 70 years old, the world found out she was an inventor. In 1997 she received the Pioneer Award from the Electronic Frontier Foundation. She died in January of 2000.

People still watch her movies. Now they know her as a great inventor and a movie star.

Hedy Lamarr, a movie star and inventor

IMPORTANT DATES TO REMEMBER

1914	Born in Vienna, Austria (November 9)
1933	Married Fritz Mandl
1937	Moved to the United States
1939	World War II began
1940	Met George Antheil
1942	Patent for Secret Communication System
1962	Navy used her weapons communication system
1997	Pioneer Award
2000	Died in Florida (January 19)

GLOSSARY

bonds (BONDZ) — papers from the government that say that if someone loans them money, the government will repay the loan with interest later

identical (eye DEN teh kel) — alike in every way

patent (PAT nt) — a grant made by the government that says only the creator of an invention has the right to make, use, or sell the invention for a period of time

player pianos (PLAY er pee AN ohz) — mechanical pianos that need no person to play the keys

satellite (SAT eh lyt) — an object that circles the Earth

submarine (sub meh REEN) — boat that goes underwater

torpedoes (tor PEE dohz) — bombs that have motors and can move themselves through the water

wireless phones (WYR liss FOHNZ) — portable telephones that operate without wires

INDEX

Further Reading

Casey, Susan. *Women Invent*! Chicago Review Press
Thimesh, Catherine. *Girls Think of Everything: Stories of Ingenious Inventions by Women.* Houghton Mifflin, 2000.

Websites To Visit

www.eff.org

About The Author

Ann Gaines is the author of many children's nonfiction books. She has also worked as a researcher in the American Civilization Program at the University of Texas.